D0359901

The editors would like to thank
BARBARA KIEFER, Ph.D.,
Charlotte S. Huck Professor of Children's Literature,
The Ohio State University, and
DANIEL C. FISHER, Ph.D.,
Curator and Director, Museum of Paleontology, University of Michigan,
for their assistance in the preparation of this book.

Visit us on the Web!
Seussville.com
randomhousekids.com

Educators and librarians, for a variety of teaching tools, visit us at
RHTeachersLibrarians.com

Library of Congress Cataloging-in-Publication Data
Worth, Bonnie, author.
Once upon a mastodon : all about prehistoric mammals / by Bonnie Worth ; illustrated by
Aristides Ruiz and Joe Mathieu. — First edition.
    pages   cm. — (The cat in the hat's learning library)
Audience: 5 to 8.
ISBN 978-0-375-87075-0 (trade) — ISBN 978-0-375-97075-7 (lib. bdg.)
1. Mammals, Fossil—Juvenile literature. 2. Glacial epoch—Juvenile literature.
I. Ruiz, Aristides, illustrator. II. Mathieu, Joe, illustrator. III. Title.
IV. Series: Cat in the Hat's learning library.
QE881.W67 2014   569—dc23   2013032532

Printed in the United States of America   10 9 8 7 6 5 4 3

Once upon a MASTODON

by Bonnie Worth

illustrated by Aristides Ruiz and Joe Mathieu

The Cat in the Hat's Learning Library®

Random House 🏠 New York

I'm the Cat in the Hat.
Oh, please turn the page
to discover some mammals
from the Great Ice Age!

Over two million years
ago in the past,
one-third of our planet
came to be frozen fast.

In the cold, many mammals
did not survive.
Others went south,
where warmth helped
them thrive.

The mammals that stayed
in the north mostly were
covered with fat
and with thick coats of fur.

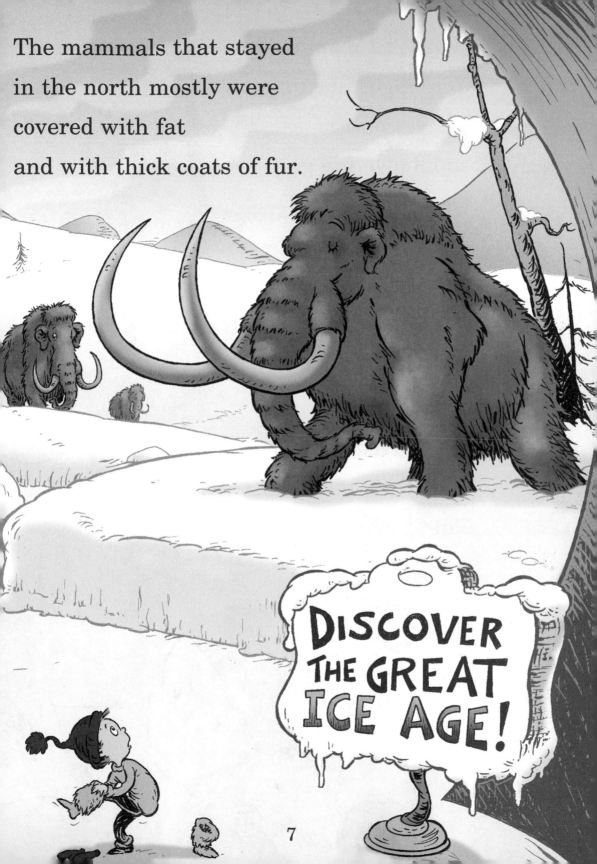

DISCOVER
THE GREAT
ICE AGE!

What is a mammal?
You might like to know.
I have some ideas,
so I'll give it a go.

A mammal is warm-blooded,
has lungs and backbone.
But there's one other trait
that I'd like to make known.

Moms feed their young milk
from their mammary glands.
That's why they're called mammals,
as I understand.

The mammals you'll see
on the tour I am giving
are extinct, which means
they are no longer living.

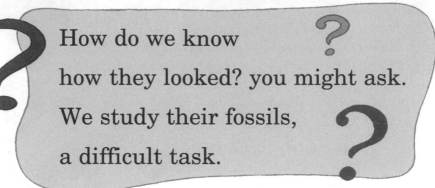

How do we know
how they looked? you might ask.
We study their fossils,
a difficult task.

Experts can guess
from very few traces

how these beasts looked
(both their bodies and faces),

CLAY

what they ate, how they moved,
and how big they grew,
if they were male or female,
and how they died, too.

Teeth, footprints, and bones
from long, long ago
are what we call fossils,
a word you may know.

The sloth of today
is the size of a cat.
But there once was a ground sloth
much bigger than that.

As big as an elephant,
it had such long claws,
it needed to walk
on the sides of its paws.

This sloth's footprints tell—
as clear as you please—
that it reared on hind legs
to munch on the trees.

Megatherium americanum

And here is a mammal,
a real crowd-pleaser,
still around at the time of the
great Julius Caesar.

With stout horns that spread
ever wider and bolder,
the aurochs stood six feet
high at the shoulder.

aurochs = AW-rox

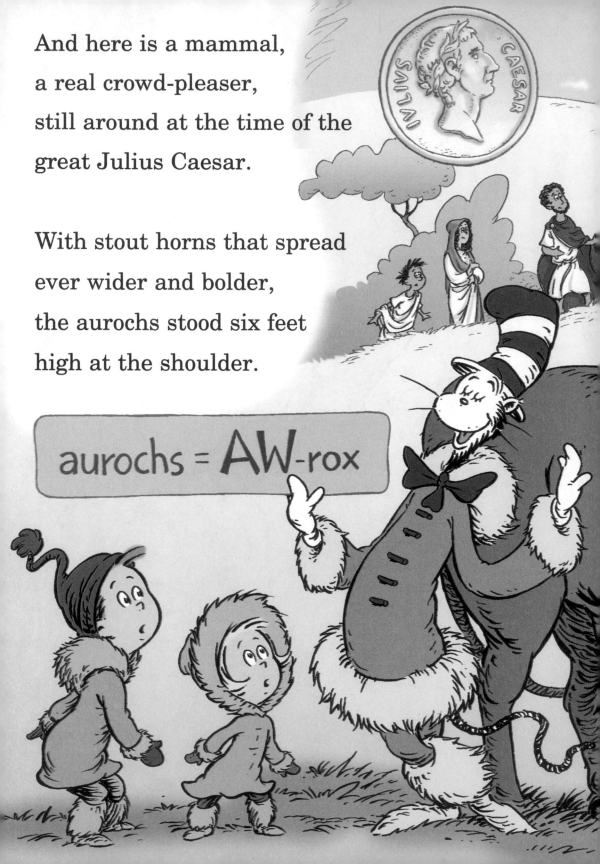

Bos primigenius

In cold North America,
on one Ice Age day,

the dire wolf here
was stalking her prey.

Her prey sank down deep
in the tar, and too late,
the dire wolf found
she had met the same fate!

Canis dirus

Come closer, my friends—
that is, if you dare—
and say hi to the giant
short-faced bear.

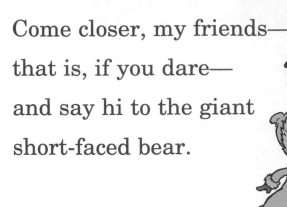

It stood ten feet tall
when on its hind feet.
Sharp teeth and strong jaw
were made to eat meat.

At two thousand pounds,
this big, furry lug
weighed almost as much as
a VW bug.

SMILE-oh-don

Having sighted a bear, we will now move on to the Great Ice Age cat we call *Smilodon*.

It had these long fangs like sabers, and that is the reason we call it a saber-toothed cat.

It hunted and scavenged—
Thing Two says it's true—
from Canada all the way
down to Peru.

Equus tau

Were there Ice Age horses?
Oh my, yes, of course—
from the pygmy on up
to what we call giant horse!

Equus pacificus

We know
of the giant
from
one single find—
a giant-sized tooth,
which boggles
the mind!

The great Irish elk,
I will state loud and clear,
holds the all-time record
for world's BIGGEST DEER!

With its antlers a whopping
twelve feet across,
it used them to show
other elks who was boss.

Bull fought with bull,
then the lucky winner
took the prize cow
on a date, out to dinner.

Megaloceros giganteus

The next mammal on deck—
oh, heed me, my son—
is the woolly one
we call the steppe bison.

Bison priscus

An Alaskan mummy
that was frozen and dried
gave us an idea
of how one bison died.

A lion tooth cracked
and was left behind.
(As fossils go,
an unusual find!)

And there on its flank,
a series of scratches
to a lion's claws
make the perfect matches!

Mammoths and mastodons,
I will now tell you kids,
belong to the order
we call proboscids.

proh - **BOS** - ids

Standing fourteen feet high,
mammoths once put away
seven hundred whole pounds
of plant matter each day.

Tusks sixteen feet long,
growing outward and curled,
made mammoth the Tusk King
of the Ice Age World.

Of mammoth fossils
there are scads and scads—
bones of the moms
and the babies and dads.

In Hot Springs, South Dakota,
sixty mammoths were found.

Where a sinkhole was,

they got stuck and drowned.

Mammoths and mastodons,
some people will claim,
with their fur, tusks,
and trunks,
were really the same.

But, shorter of tusk
and with legs
not as long,
mastodon
was smaller,
though still
plenty strong.

Mammoth's skull
was domed
and mastodon's flat,
but the difference,
you see,
goes well beyond that.

Mammut americanum

32

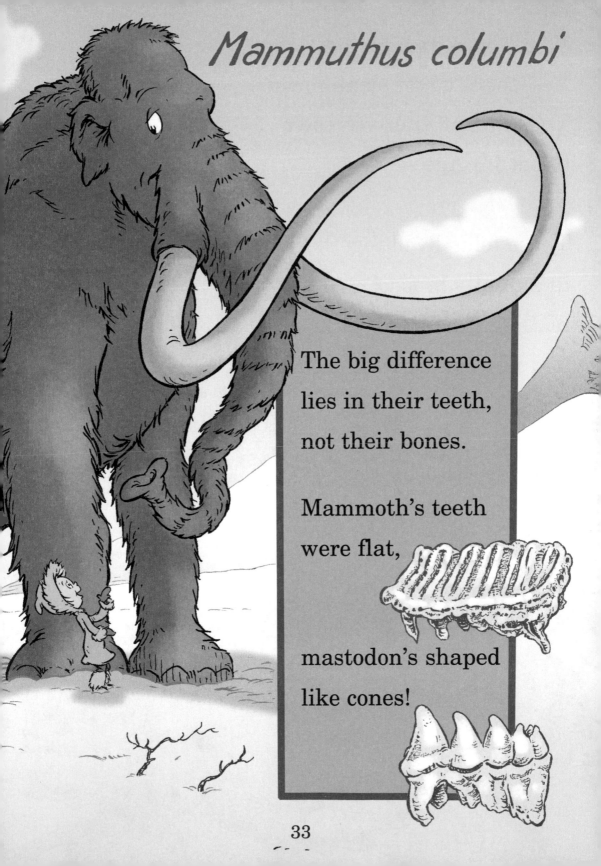

Mammuthus columbi

The big difference
lies in their teeth,
not their bones.

Mammoth's teeth
were flat,

mastodon's shaped
like cones!

Were there humans back then?
Yes, there were, by all means!
The stars of their very own
Great Ice Age scenes!

These folks lived together
in a family brood,
making fire for warmth
and for cooking their food.

They gathered up fruit
and roots, nuts, and seeds
and killed to get meat
and for their other needs.

The Ice Age worker
who is pictured here
is chipping flint points
to tie on to his spear.

They were not just hunters,
men brave of heart.
These Stone Age people
were skilled at art.

From stones and shells
and dried-up seeds,
they made headdresses
and strings of beads.

With a flute carved of bone
or an empty conch shell,
they would make music,
and some danced as well.

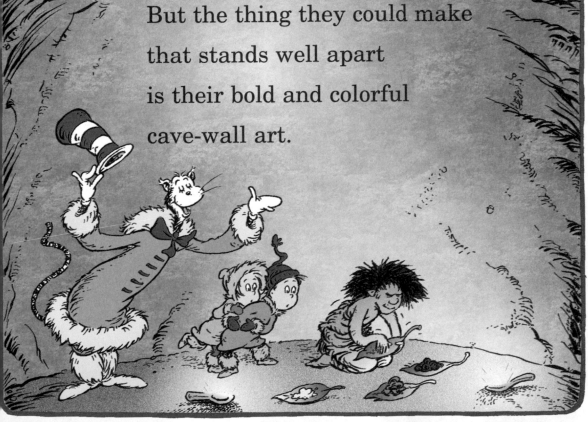

But the thing they could make
that stands well apart
is their bold and colorful
cave-wall art.

These great works of art
are still being found
on walls inside caves
deep under the ground.

In colors and lines
these Stone Agers drew
the Ice Age mammals
they hunted and slew.

Such beautiful pictures,
as you can see here:
rhino, mammoth, bison,
lion, bear, and deer.

But the one
missing mammal
that I'd like to see
in a bold cave-wall picture
is little old . . .

GLOSSARY

Brood: A family of young animals or people.

Conch: A kind of a large sea snail.

Gland: An organ in the body that releases chemical substances.

Julius Caesar: A famous general and leader of ancient Rome, who was born a hundred years before the birth of Christ.

Prey: An animal caught and eaten by a predator for food.

Proboscideans: Animals belonging to the order that includes the elephant and many extinct species, like the woolly mammoth.

Saber: A sword with a slightly curved blade.

Sinkhole: A natural depression or hole in the earth caused by a collapse of the surface layer, usually brought about by groundwater dissolving lower layers of rock.

Steppe: Flat lands in southeastern Europe and Asia that have few trees.

Tusks: Long, continuously growing front teeth that stick out of the mouths of certain animals.

FOR FURTHER READING

Discovery in the Cave by Mark Dubowski, illustrated by Bryn Barnard (Random House, *Step into Reading, Step 4*). Four boys and a dog discover the most famous prehistoric paintings in the world! For grades 2–4.

Early Humans (DK Publishing, *DK Eyewitness Books*). A look at the world of ancient people and their way of life. Illustrated with photographs. For ages 8 and up.

The First Dog by Jan Brett (Harcourt Brace & Company, *Voyager Books*). A lushly illustrated imaginary story about how the first wild animal might have been domesticated during the Ice Age. For ages 4–8.

Mammoths and Mastodons: Titans of the Ice Age by Cheryl Bardoe (Abrams). This award-winning book explores the latest theories about how mammoths and mastodons lived. With photographs and illustrations. For grades 4–7.

Wild and Woolly Mammoths by Aliki (HarperCollins). A beloved children's book author explains how mammoths lived, what they ate, and how they survived. For ages 4–8.

INDEX

The Cat in the Hat's Learning Library

The Cat in the Hat's Learning Library

The Cat in the Hat's Learning Library

The Cat in the Hat's Learning Library

The Cat in the Hat's Learning Library

The Cat in the Hat's Learning Library

The Cat in the Hat's Learning Library

The Cat in the Hat's Learning Library

The Cat in the Hat's Learning Library

The Cat in the Hat's Learning Library

The Cat in the Hat's Learning Library

The Cat in the Hat's Learning Library

The Cat in the Hat's Learning Library

The Cat in the Hat's Learning Library

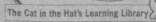
The Cat in the Hat's Learning Library